Rebecca Jessup's poetry is deeply spiritual and also worldly-wise, rich with detailed, insightful, telling observation. Her poems are beautiful, as immediate and accessible as beautiful music.
  —Dave Edgerton, author of the novel *270 EAST*

Rebecca's poems have the kind human sensitivity and attunement that makes you feel deeply connected to other people, other lives, other experiences — each poem a portal, with details so rich and distinct that they live in you for years.
  —Laine Kuehn, poet
  and member of one of Rebecca's poetry groups.

Rebecca's poems are infused with a classical grace and thrill of language. They ground the uplift of formal lyricism with daily, earthly detail. They sing. This collection reads almost like a love poem to poetry itself. Bold, adept and reverent.
  —Barbaria Maria, poet
  and head of one of Rebecca's poetry groups

Our dear friend, Rebecca Jessup, in her final chapbook, **Sorrows End**, *goes to the places of deepest mourning. From wild interpretations of Biblical texts, to an astounding philosophy of poetry, to love's upheavals, to family as sacred ground, to gardens, where when she went digging, the words and flowers and vegetables all bloomed together. In an Audubon tree park in Kentucky with cathedral bird overtones she is asserting: Everything is a poem. Her poems essentially say, "I want to be a dear friend of everything."*

—Elizabeth Garber, former Belfast Poet Laureate

Sorrows End

Rebecca Jessup

Goose River Press
Waldoboro, Maine

Copyright © 2023 Rebecca Jessup

All rights reserved. No part of this book may be reproduced in any form without written permission from the publisher, except by a reviewer who may quote brief passages in a review to be printed in a newspaper or magazine.

Library of Congress Card Number: 2023940587

ISBN: 978-1-59713-264-0

Cover photo of "Carol's Garden" New Harmony, Indiana by Docey Lewis.

Second Printing, 2023

.

Published by
Goose River Press
3400 Friendship Road
Waldoboro ME 04572
e-mail: gooseriverpress@gmail.com
www.gooseriverpress.com

Dedicated to Duncan

Because this would never have come about without him.

Table of Contents

I Poems of Place
    Southern Indiana, Late Fall   1
    Audubon Park   2
    Maine   3
    Comeback   4
    Storm in Bay   6
    Returning   7
    The Middle East   8

II Poems of Mourning
    After Death   11
    Death Changes the World: A Report on Conditions   12
    Mother   13

III Poems with Biblical References
    To Ruth From Her Mother   17
    Long After, Eve Returns   19
    Earth-like Planet Discovered Only 20-Light-years Away   21

IV Poems From or About Poetry
    Riffing on Shakespeare 30   27
    The Breakdown Lane   29
    Shame and Poetry   30
    What Is Poetry (With Notes on What It Isn't)   31
    It's a Poem   34
    Unwritten Poems   35
    Dactyls   36

Table of Contents

V Love's Upheavals

Careless Love and the Old Dam Road   41
Looking for a Place   42
What We Dared   44

VI Family

Raised on Mount Olympus   47
Reprehensible   49
The Reason for a Kitten   51
Fragments   52
Precious: To My Late Mother   54
Home Grown   55

VII Gardens

Alcyon Cherry Tomatoes   59
Rubus Fruticosus   60
Post Lapsarian   61
Unripe Saints   62

Rebecca completed her work on this chapbook while Poet in Residence at The Poets House in New Harmony, Indiana. She was always grateful to the Blaffer Foundation, and to Docey Lewis, in New Harmony, for their sponsorship.

Sorrows End

I

Poems of Place

Southern Indiana, Late Fall

We heard that the first hard frost
Would hit last night.
Today I looked out early
For any touch of white,

For rime on leaves or grass,
Or ice on windowpanes.
One stubborn pink geranium
On its jaunty, slender cane

Refused to fall or grow old
But stretched out in dawning light.
She seemed to defy the cold,
Awaiting full daylight.

Gardens were put to bed,
Tomato vines plowed under.
This one defiant head
Refused to founder.

Audubon Park

We walked into the woods
and the trees were higher than cathedrals,
with warty-trunked yellow orange spires,
with grapevine flying buttresses,
and low shots of bright red among the pews of fallen trunks,
lit by distant leafy lancets,
spotted with layers of mottled mushrooms,
fungus striped like snail shells,
as surprising and inevitable as butterfly wings,
and the muddy earth covered with brown leaves,
neon-yellow leaves, orange leaves,
butter-yellow leaves, green leaves,
summer-yellow leaves, leaves as small as thumbnails,
leaves as wide as birthday cakes.
We saw trees sweeping down the hollow of a hill,
there were rivulets in the cracks and gullies,
unlikely footbridges made through some anonymous kind
                                                                industry,
and then the treed ground swooped up
and all we could hear was wind in the high, high trees,
and sometimes from on high
the antiphonal choirs of birds.

Maine

January chill arrives so sharp, so
certain of itself, no thickness of wood or glass,
no straw-bales dull or muffle
its footfall. There is no mistaking it,
no deception, no disguising it. Nothing
fends it off. We are scarcely safe.
Through whitening glass panes
we watch its unhesitant, indifferent advance,
gliding over the dense woods,
the black, binding roads. Even along the coast
the softening love of our shared mother ocean
hardens. Floes bestill the bay, and glaze the cove.

Comeback

This is the time for writing; sun's just up
and dawn light color on the bay has dimmed
orange to pink. The bay is quiet, calm,
the island visible through branches, leaves,
the island a dark, lumpen ribbon that
splits water from its mirror sky. We have
just arrived here. The island's name is still
not quick to come to mind. I still can trip
on unexpected stair. Nothing is yet
familiar in my bones except the air,
the smell, the latitude and longitude,
the calls, the songs, the accents of these birds,
the heft, the skin-bark texture, birch, and pine,
and oak trees, rasping, scraping branch on branch
and shining tin-like under northern light,
the bluing shades of lupines, and white blooms
that yield to fruit by August every year.
It isn't just the bright remembered times
of every childhood summer, nor the weight
and clarity of sea salt in the air,
the smack of dead low tide and sea worn glass,
nor seaweed, shells decaying into sand.
It is the thrill and humbling certainty
that these Atlantic waters that I watch
from green-trimmed windows or from porch
have all the force they have forever had.
Last night they raged up toward us with the tide,
roiling whitecaps, notifying me
that they could still, on any day or night,
rip out the pilings, piers and solid docks,
the riprap stones, the new, expensive homes,

(continued)

the old stone ramparts, new retaining walls,
the road that brought me here. Drowning is one
fine way to die, if water wills it so.
Now the deceptive, sleepy waters doze,
but they awe me still. They always have.
They always will. That's all the god I have.

Storm in Bay

Waves in frothy disarray
wash and swoosh across the bay
yanked by tide and whipped by gale
whitecaps like thick head on ale
rush before the strafing wind
roar above the ocean's din.
Heaving storm winds fling and toss
leaves and branches zing across
roads and gulley, up and down,
shout inhuman forest sounds —
whooshing, tumbling, then a crash,
thudding, falling, branch on branch.
Creatures flee their tumbling home,
as storm pitch falls from scream to groan.
In the morning, chill and gray
wavelets pass on calm display.

Returning

This is a safe house, on loan.
Our weeks here stretch out in front of us,
still immaculate.

Old wooden floors, beams, windowsills,
floors slightly a-kilter, windowpanes rippled.
I am curious, charmed, exploring
drawers, closets, cupboards — putting clothes and soap away,
searching for soupspoons. Outside, look —
trees barely in bud, yellow daffodils and forsythia,
spring winds, river in low flood.

Look, the bridge is still closed. That great, gray sycamore is gone,
                                                                            but
look, friends are still here.
In the joy of reunion, laughter's deep register voices for us
what words can't plumb.

The Middle East

Nothing is fun, easy or fair.
Nothing young, simple, true.
Is anything kind, civil, rare?
No one flawless, youthful, new.
Nowhere safe, not safe enough.
Nothing straightforward or bare.
No one innocent, Gentile or Jew.
Every surface weathered and rough.

What stair do you stand on?
Which hand do you raise?
No answer, no word is simple.
Every letter has numbers, symbols, secrets
impossible to construe. Clothing holds meaning—
made of what material? How deep is black? Nothing is
only what it seems. Everything
is more, less, more or less. Nothing is
what it was yesterday, last week, or
this morning. No one has changed, no one moved, but
nothing is where it was. We do just as we
always do, but
nothing is quite what it was.

Here, water flows rarely, only in winter.
And who can say where
is downhill, anyway.

(Inspired by Alan Dugan, I and Thou, "Nothing is plumb, level or square.")

II

Poems of Mourning

After Death

Since you died, I have woken every day.
That has been the hardest part, that instant
when you have to be deadened again—
not killed, but given back to death.
I smother that hopeful sense
that clings to me from sleep.
I send you back across, or I cross, myself,
the swirling black that swims around the dream.

This is only a matter of seconds.
Then the day proceeds.
This is the real work of the day.
The rest, routine.

Death Changes the World: A Report on Conditions

Brother, you died twenty days ago.
The world now is angrier, more populous, busier,
narrower in streets and in prospects.
The sky is lower, more cluttered.
Kindness and safety have diminished.
Babbling languages, incomprehensible, have multiplied.
Poverty increases, and rumors gain speed.

Mother

In, out. In, out.
I learned to breathe (in, out) from you.
(In, out) there inside where air wasn't,
I heard (in, out) you breathe, through
the black warm liquid slosh (in, out).
I in earliest reptilian stage learned (in, out)
to breathe, the ocean's beat.

I breathe in, breathe out. My daughter breathes.
She so flamboyantly self-willed, she
also breathes in, breathes out. But not you. Not you.
I force myself to know this.
Your breathing days are gone.
That warm, ocean body, generous like you,
stopped breathing in, out. Has gone.
Cremated. Is now cinder, ash.

I breathe in, out, as you did.
But you are not here. I search and search.
Some urgent rhythm is gone. I search and flail.
Your child is breathing (in, out)
And grieving, grieving.

III

Poems with Biblical References

To Ruth From Her Mother
And Boaz answered and said unto her, It has fully been shown me, all that you have done unto your mother-in-law since the death of your husband: and how you have left your father and your mother, and the land of your birth, and are come unto a people which you knew not before. The Lord recompense your work, and a full reward be given you of the Lord God of Israel, under whose wings you have come to trust.
— Ruth 2:11–12 KJV

Your father met a herder on Traders Way.
He said you have been widowed, that Mahlon and Elimelech are
                                                                                                   dead,
and you have taken a new husband among the Israelites,
taken a new god. Taken Mahlon's mother.

Mahlon and Elimelech are dead, but you
do not come to my side to grieve with me,
you do not turn to me for comfort as you
did when you were small, when I held you.

I grieve alone for you, my child, grieve
for your loss, grieve for the death of your young husband,
grieve that you cannot, will not return to me now,
grieve that you have left us to our loss,

in our age, abandoned us to our sorrow.
The herder has no word for us from you,
no word of comfort or remembrance,
no word of longing or of love.

Do you not feel my love, my grief?
Did you and I not fall in love at your birth, exhausted and
                                                          astonished?
Did I not feed you at my fat breast,
feed you my milk, my love, my worship?

Your children will never stand with me
to sing prayers before Ashtar-Chemosh, as you
did with my mother, you a small wondering girl,
folding yourself into her skirts, as I did with her mother in Gilead.

The herder says your new husband
is wealthy, and praises you, that you have left
your mother and father to go into Israel,
left the nation of your birth, left your gods.

In that strange land you are praised for hard, cruel deeds,
for coldness toward your bent mother, your sorrowing father.
You may turn from us forever, but some among Jesse's line will
                                                              have
my mother's perfect high-arched foot, my father's eyes.

Long After, Eve Returns

Somehow I have slipped back in,
crept past the gentlest cherub
and the spinning, flaming swords.
The animals remember me,
the leopard, the gray wolf, the gazelle
stroll over to nuzzle greetings, ask me
how I am, to thank me for their names.
The jackal laughs and tugs my hand,
elephants sway and swing their trunks;
the larks and hamsters chatter so loudly
that I hush them.
                      My time is short,
and I should not have come.
Since Abel died, and Cain went away,
I know far better what it means to be cursed,
to lose a home, to lose a child.
See the baby antelope: it will stay
near its mother all its life. See the
lion-cub brothers; they will wander
forever, never lose each other.
Even as they learn to kill,
they will never kill each other.
Oh, could I not have been made, instead,
from the rib of the great lion?
Sweet parakeet, brave owl, lively hoopoe,
friend turtle, how I miss you, out in the hard
world! Oh my beloveds, do remember me!
Visit me in dreams, bring
me news and comfort!
                        May I never again
lay eyes on that damned tree—but oh, this spot,

                                              (continued)

this flat soft place in the high grass where first
Adam lay with me! Oh, the pool here where we
drank each morning, the orchard where we slept!
Oh my beloveds, visit me in dreams!
Bring me your news, your memories!
Adam and God declare that it was all my doing,
as though I had had choice but Adam none.
That is how he sees it, how he always will. As though
the game were fair.
                               But now the cherubim have heard
us; they come with the flaming swords, chase me away.

Earth-like Planet Discovered Only 20 Light-years Away

So that's it, then, we have our destination.
    Get the kinks worked out—perpetual fuel sources,
        ship, indestructible—size of a modest asteroid, perhaps—

set it spinning in orbit, like the space station,
    select a few strong blood-lines, perfect genomes,
        a pool of seeds and spores, sperms and eggs,

and listen, we're all set! Ready in our ordered lines,
    we lucky, precious hundreds, ruthlessly selected,
        we'll board this modern ark, aim it at that new Ararat,

and, look, by the time the oceans' average temperatures
    have far exceeded all predictions
        we'll be ready to launch, trained, equipped,

smart enough, healthy, even wise, why not—
    youthful and strong, with solid plans, drilled, rehearsed.
        We'll have laid in supplies, we'll have counted down.

We'll feel the lurch as we leave earth's pull,
    and through the portholes we'll see
        the shapely Atlantic, or the once-crystalline Caribbean, or

the beautiful barrier reef, now gray
    with the flotsam of sunken islands,
        sour with dead mammals—humans and whales.

The asteroid-ship will pulse and we'll each pray good-bye
    to corners we have known, I to the knotty-pine Maine cabin
        wall, she to the Parthenon, he to one particular rice paddy,

they to a grandfather's stone hut in Tibet, to the view from there,
    someone to the winter lake winds of Chicago,
        another to rushing Victoria Falls, someone else to the last

giraffe in Africa, the last Russian bear.
    To each our own lost Edens. Oh, views from the roofs of Paris!
        Oh, the slums of Bangladesh, Lagos, Sao Paulo!

All of it recorded, all documented, all backed up,
    all memorialized for some maybe future
        when our ever-so-great grandchildren

need to explain themselves, where they came from,
    having grown up knowing—what? Whatever they will about
        about what Earth was, that it was perfect, but

destroyed, allowed to die, that it was
    glorious, but we, their ancestors,
        we despoiled our nest, spoiled

air and water, killed off our fellows, even
    our food supply, burned ourselves and each other up
        killed off our neighborhoods—

For what? Some will ask.
    What were they thinking? Some will ask.
        Why? They will want to know.

For greed, we'd have to say. For progress,
    someone will joke. Think about it.
        Some denied, derided thoughts of what was happening.

Some thought that God was in charge, would make it right.
    Some that another, extra-terrestrial, race would save us.
        Some thought we would become angels, flying to new
                                worlds.

Many of us, in every city and coffee shop,
    resisted, wrote letters, marched, recycled,
        composted, rode bicycles, grew food, organized.

We were outgunned. We won't know why.
    We won't remember. It was so many, many
        generations gone. Within the asteroid, by that time,

human nature being what it is, what it always has been,
    we will have started, suffered, and survived
        any number of wars by then.

IV

Poems From or About Poetry

Riffing on Shakespeare 30

SONNET 30

When to the sessions of sweet silent thought
I summon up remembrance of things past,
I sigh the lack of many a thing I sought,
And with old woes new wail my dear time's waste:
Then can I drown an eye, unus'd to flow,
For precious friends hid in death's dateless night,
And weep afresh love's long since cancell'd woe,
And moan the expense of many a vanish'd sight:
Then can I grieve at grievances foregone,
And heavily from woe to woe tell o'er
The sad account of fore-bemoaned moan,
Which I new pay as if not paid before.
But if the while I think on thee, dear friend,
All losses are restor'd and sorrows end.
— William Shakespeare

Sometimes

Sometimes I love to be quiet, and remember old times.
Sometimes I get sad, remembering sad times,
people I loved who have died,
people and places I've lost,
hard times, regrets,
old broken hearts.
Sometimes one old sad memory
just leads on to another even sadder.
Sometimes I cry all over again,
as though all those sad times
were happening now, all of them piled together.

(continued)

Sometimes I can cry and cry,
as though I'd never cried before,
cried them all out a long time ago.
Sometimes I can fall back
into those old griefs like into a deep pit,
feel old wounds as hard and sharp as a new knife,
as present and dangerous as a loaded gun—
and each old loss still hurts like hell.
But then, sometimes, I think of you.
And right then, I have everything.
Right then all old sorrows just end. They end.

The Breakdown Lane
(With apologies to Yeats)

Politics

How can I, that girl standing there,
My attention fix
On Roman or on Russian
Or on Spanish politics?
Yet here's a travelled man that knows
What he talks about,
And there's a politician
That has read and thought,
And maybe what they say is true
Of war and war's alarms,
But O that I were young again
And held her in my arms!

—W.B. Yeats

How can I, with you sitting there,
Turn my mind's direction
To stoplights or yield lanes
or three-way intersections?
Yet here's a tricky traffic spot,
Cars merging, with a blind turn,
And there's a yellow caution sign.
Just there's a cop all set to churn,
Spit gravel in a roaring chase,
With flashers and alarms,
But oh, that we were home somewhere
And in each other's arms!

Shame and Poetry

Shame

I had some success in the beginning —
but I discounted it, felt I was only
inhaling and exhaling, like everyone else. Nothing
I said, nothing I did could be called rare or lovely,
intricate, subtle, or finely wrought. It was just that I
stepped into such-and-such a room, on
such-and-such a day, and saw and did what
anyone would have seen and done, and said
only what anyone might have said.

Poetry

The task, the trick, the challenge is this:
to remove myself from my own accounting,
to call myself *she* or *you*,
to shield against, deflect the harshest light,
turn it back, mirror it so that you
are sitting where I sit, feeling
what we all feel.

What Is Poetry (With Notes on What It Isn't)

I have listened to many poets and many poems lately,
and I have learned this.

Poetry is whatever did or didn't happen,
wherever you went or didn't go,
whatever you thought or hoped or wished,
or whatever you didn't and don't
think, or hope, or wish.

If you woke early and watched the sun rise,
that's a poem.
If you had lively dreams, or nightmares,
or a vision of your dead friend,
that's a poem.
If you slept long and deep and silent,
that's a poem.

When you walk down a city street,
every person you pass is a poem—
the old woman who limps,
the little girl who skips past her parents' reach,
the baby carriage, the skater,
the rude, loud boys, laughing and running—
they're all poems.

When you swim in the cold lake or the cold salt sea,
or the crowded chlorine pool,
that's a poem.
If you used to dive and swim and dance, but you can't anymore,
that's a poem.
Whatever you remember about this place
or about any other place
whatever you do now
or used to do, or hope to do,
or wish you had done
is a poem.

What you've forgotten,
the people, their names,
or their faces, or
the little events that tied them to you
or that didn't,
that's a poem.

Poetry is whatever is and whatever is not—
a loon or a whale or a phoenix,
roses, or a cat in a tree, or a magic wand,
your father's sister, or the goddesses on Mount Olympus,
whatever you know or know about,
or think you know, or wish you knew,
that's a poem.

If you fall in love, that's at least a volume of poems.
(*Fall   in   love*
is a three-word
poem easy to remember,
impossible to know.)
If you rise in hate,
write it, write it,
it's a poem.
It's a poem.
Don't let it be anything less.
Don't let it be anything more.

A poem is not a commercial, not a TV show,
not a sitcom,
not "to be continued …."
A poem doesn't glare at you from
a green-blue screen,
doesn't conspire to sell you or buy you.
Poetry may not be factual
but poetry is truth.

You don't have to wait for it,
you just have to write it.
That is what I've learned. If I had known this sooner,
I would have written
oh, so many poems!

It's a Poem

I know that a poem
may come
should come
will come.
I know by the fluttering surge
that is welling up in my chest
expelling air in a long sigh
so that I breathe in a deep gasp
swelling my heart.
It is not about you or me or love.
It is not about morning or the sunlight through the shutters.
It is not about last night or last week or tomorrow.
It is not about the autumn-colored cat who, minutes ago,
whimpered, peeked out at us, ran wildly away.
It is not about my dead mother, or my dead brother, or a dead
                                                                              friend.
It is not about the seeds I that I have poked prayerfully into
                                        sequestered squares of dirt.
It is not about the cold outside
or the ice that has grown half way up the windowpanes.
The poem is about nothing
but the sensation of a poem
pushing to be born.

Unwritten Poems

The ether is so full of them, as full
as the night is full of snowflakes. They
swarm and fly and dance, the unwritten poems,
and blink out like dying stars, or rather like those tiny
fireflies, that shine when they rise, then
dim and darken as they fall. Tell me
what became of the wave
that we watched swelling in the bay
this morning, after it splashed and splattered?
No two are alike—no two of anything are alike.
None of the unwritten poems or songs will ever be seen
or heard, except perhaps by God. The most beautiful poems never
                                                              written
are lost, the loveliest songs never heard are lost.
How beautiful they were, in their
secret night lifetimes!
How beautiful they were!

Dactyls

Dactyls are waltzable, oom-pa-pa syllables,
Sometimes they're much too loud—
Jackhammers, lawn mowers,
Car alarms, leaf blowers,
Ambulance, cop sirens,
Noises like that.

Sometimes they're beautiful—
Butterflies, Saturdays,
Celebrate holidays,
Maple trees, sycamores,
Lumbering elephants,
Tri-cornered hats.

Whatever shall we do?
(Scan that one carefully!)
Someone, oh, somebody
(That's an apostrophe,
maybe anaphora)
Give us a roadmap or
something like that.

From the Encyclopedia Britannica:
Dactyl, metrical foot consisting of one long (classical verse) or stressed (English verse) syllable followed by two short, or unstressed, syllables. Probably the oldest and most common metre in classical verse is the dactylic hexameter, the metre of Homer's Iliad and Odyssey and of other ancient epics.
http://www.britannica.com/EBchecked/topic/149471/dactyl

Note: Dactyl is Greek for finger (or toe). Fingers, like dactyls, can be seen as having three parts—the first being longer, and the latter two being shorter. This little verse is dactylic in the English sense, not the Latin or Greek sense. And although each line has two dactyls, it is not properly a double dactyl, also known as a Higgledy-Piggledy.

Previously published in *Classical Outlook*, Fall 2013

V

Love's Upheavals

Careless Love and the Old Dam Road

This love swept through like a tornado.
This love ripped up house, marriage, friends
sent me barreling through swirling air currents
like a witch on a bicycle, climbing the whirlwind,
flinging papers, gardens, commitments, whole towns aside
like so much chalk dust, like so much salt flung over your
                                                            shoulder,
leaving no recognizable order, no sense,
only a terrible job of work to be done,
work to recalibrate, work to re-establish
some safety, some history
some new life out of the ruins.

All this so that you and I could turn by chance
onto a canopied green dirt road,
drive through a thickly wooded hollow and
walk over dust-dirt drive, walk half way across a wide, rippling
                                                                             river
on a sedimentary rock shelf,
feel the current's breeze on our faces,
see the waters flowing toward us, past us and away,
point at the dozens of bugs hovering over the water,
spot the almond-sized fish breaking the surface in crazy hops,
notice a white-muzzled beagle, nose to the ground, eyes on us,
trotting along the bank.

Published in *Posey Magazine,* Jan-Feb 2013, pg. 23
http://issuu.com/poseymagazine/docs/posey_magazinejan-feb13?e=1986399/2521444

Looking for a Place
For Richard J. Margolis

I am trying to find —
I am hoping to find —
I am looking for a place,
for a place for my things,
some place for my things,
things I have brought with me,
brought with me for a long time.

Looking for —
hoping to find —
seeking some quarter, some station,
where inert things,
the relics of the dear
dead and the long forgotten dead
can take root
and push out buds
and grow. Because why else —
why else would I —
why else have I carried, do I carry
these old linen napkins,
this silver bowl, these dried-out papers,
this engraved mirror,

when so many things
have been lost,
have fallen into indifferent hands,
have been sold, thrown violently away,
have been auctioned off
like the slaves they were.

Auctioned like slaves, without thought
for their lives, their meanings,
their history, parents, children.

I am the child, or grandchild, or some long-string leftover
of the owners of these last shreds of things,
these remaining slaves. These last
are too broken, too dear, too old to sell.
My distant grandmothers, proud and pleased,
held these things and passed them on,
forgetting, if they ever knew,
that owning a slave is in itself a bondage.

Those remote women that I love,
whose names were in that auctioned Bible —
whose small, square, framed and blackened daguerreotype

                                                                               images

were lost to greed, to estate battles, probate wars —
they bequeathed me these things, their last, loved slaves,
and bonded me to them.

I am looking for a place,
for a place for my things
where my things can grow roots
and push out sky-reaching branches
and become a place —
a place for my grandmothers,
a place for me.

What We Dared

Some inner beast and I
have dared to leave the hearth—

leave it with no way back,
leave it with the hope

that we would find or make
some new hearth over the mountain

up in a cave or
under a tree.

Hope that the next hearth would have
warmth, food, water. We dared to hope

because the hearth would surely
follow the heart

and the heart of the inner beast
is loud and great.

V

Family

Raised on Mount Olympus

I was raised on Mount Olympus.
Many of us were.
We toddled, grew, played in a high-walled marble nursery
where deity parents would sometimes visit
when they could, between wars and storms of vengeance,
between crashing love affairs and undulating, surging
                                       earthquakes.
Gods and goddesses, alone or in pairs,
would stop and visit, watching us.

We played with spent lightning bolts,
snacked on biscuits of nectar,
drank leftover ambrosia
which sweet Vesta would pour into the soup
along with the barley and lentils.
Bacchus, when he swaggered in,
turned the soup to a strong, dark mead, sang loud,
sloshed wine from his pockets and collar, everywhere,
left stains on the marble floors
and waltzed us all around, bellowing handsomely,
not knowing, not curious which or how many of us
might be his.
We laughed and sang, ran rings around him, and loved —
ever on guard for ourselves, for each other,
on guard against his carelessly swinging, outstretched arms,
his dangerous hilarity.
No one claimed him father.

We assumed that Jupiter
had sired nearly all of us.
He was so massive, so strong and compelling,
eyebrows like fallen pine trees.

He came to the nursery twice,
and twice I thought I saw him nod,
that sign of approval which we all knew to covet and to fear.

Born above the cloud mists,
there was no height for us to aim for,
and we were rudderless, aimed only vaguely down, we supposed.
Silently we wished a desperate hope
that we were really the children
of nameless, rankless mortals;
that we had been left there as foundlings,
quite by mistake.

Reprehensible

Can I reach that dead branch? I stretch both arms,
    one hand grasps the branch, the other clips it,
        as far down as I can reach, close to the trunk.

Reprehensible, that at this age
    that she has built no monuments,
        never found any adult footing.

Lilacs shed so much! So many dead twigs,
    and the remains of old blossoms. I cut many branches
        with no new sap or life, send them lifeless to the ground.

No adult footing, no fiscal sense,
    she'll be a drain on her kids.
        a taker, a drain on us all.

There is a sad finality in each clip, each cut. After the lilac,
    an aging apple tree that leans over the ditch. Deadwood
        so thick and brittle it snaps and falls, scattershot.

To re-prehend means to hold, grasp back, to grasp again.
    Or so it should mean. Somehow it becomes
        to charge, to blame. How we love blame!

It pleases me to free the trees of their dead parts. I imagine
    that the lilac tree, the apple trunk feel relief, freed, as though
                finally
        someone had clipped their overgrown toenails and straggly
                      hair.

The thrum of family gossip rumbles just below
   the range of human hearing. Judgment is its
       percussion, sorrow the score.

Once I was called the owner of a house, trees, land. No more.
   Someone else holds title here, and there.
       Still, these branches call to me to trim, to help.

Apprehend, comprehend.
   Prehensile. Comprehensive.
       Apprehensive. Reprehensible.

I know that trees can sing, and can weep. There are some who can
                                                         hear them.
   Perhaps they cry out a little when I snip off the dying twigs.
   Perhaps they sense that I love them.

The Reason for a Kitten

During her last year,
my mother was alone a lot
except for her friendly, nameless kitten.
Kitten hopped and danced, comically, as kittens do,
and my mother laughed and laughed.
Kitten slept beside her, even though
my mother was old, and smelled of urine.
When my mother died, kitten was a young cat
who, the day before we held the sale,
gave birth to five kittens, even though
we were all gathered, fractious, sullen, unhappy.
A neighbor took her, kittens and all,
and named her Momma Cat, proclaimed her to be
especially sensitive, especially sweet.

Momma Cat and her kits
have all died of old age years ago.
Still, I can hear my mother laughing at her play,
both of them surprised, distracted, wonder-filled — even though
my mother was old, and dying, and otherwise alone.

Fragments

Life is not so long
if you slice it into segments of,
say, fifteen years.

First fifteen for childhood — parents, siblings, first homes,
pets, nicknames, forever-long summers,
earliest terrors.

A few years' break, then fifteen more for first marriage,
childbirth, babies, carpools, some experiments in work,
experiments in self.

Fifteen is enough, surely a good-faith effort —
how can you be faulted for a failure
after fifteen years?

Scratch together fifteen here and there
to single life, custody, college, friendships,
vocation, losses, storms at sea.

Give fifteen to marriage number two,
some form of career, teenagers, accidents,
entertaining, coffee groups.

And pretty soon, you're near the end.
You can see the finish line from here.
Parents are long gone, friends are starting

to vanish into the impenetrable. Kids
are vibrantly absent, all their lively interest
focused somewhere else. And you're looking back

at broken mirrors, shards of time, life scattered in
bits here and pieces there, held together only
by you, the rememberer. Those individual, shattering

choices that felt inevitable have left
a crazy mosaic. Friends from this chapter never met
lovers from that first volume.

You can still see every knothole in that narrow staircase that they
                                                                                                  tore down,
but you're never entirely certain now of the latest steps and
                                                                                                    contours,
or exactly how you came to this room.

Precious: To My Late Mother

I thought that I loved you
because you were the prettiest of the mothers
because you taught me to sing, and more,
to sing as lustily as those who sang better than I did
because you knew the names of all the kings of England
and, just as quickly, the names of all my dolls
because you sat and instructed me
in the rhythms of spondees and iambs
because you let me read Katharine
at least in Act One
when I was fourteen
because you made up
songs for us that only we knew
or perhaps because I had learned to breathe
there in your whale-belly
from your in breath, from your exhale.

It was all of these and it was none of these things.
I loved you because
you saw me as some kind of precious,
precious first, precious last, precious always.
I could never lose that knowledge. I could never
barter it away. I am precious to you.
I am precious to you.
I am precious.

Home Grown

In these parts people settle close to home.
Families live all their lives in one small town.
You almost never hear of children gone
off to some distant place; they stick around.
Mothers and fathers, children, siblings, here
they live, they argue, splinter and unite
for barbecues, some supper and a beer,
to watch each other's kids, to spend the night,
to talk about each other, to critique
somebody's recent date or latest car,
to hear each other's voices, just to speak,
to say "I'm down the street, I'm never far."

They don't send off their young as pioneers
to conquer far-off unexplored frontiers.
They join for joy or mourning, all in reach.
They sing, like mermaids, each to each to each.

(NB – This was originally meant to be a sonnet, but I was unwilling to sacrifice either of the final couplets for the sake of the form.)

VII

Gardens

Alcyon Cherry Tomatoes

I have longed to grow
those tangy, spitfire, kicky little globes,
but I have failed, gathering only a handful,
embarrassingly few, of this fruit
said to be foolproof.
Now I am here, helping to put someone else's garden
to bed for the winter. So many, scores
and scores of the red balls and yellow balls, heaping,
piles, burying themselves into the dirt.
Cats' eyes, agates, shooters, in yellows, orange and reds.
And there are many more, brimming in bowls, indoors.
Down the path an apple tree has dumped
a wide, misshapen circle overflowing with yellow apples,
like a spiral galaxy of stars and planets, fallen carelessly to
ground. I want to redistribute this true wealth.
I want to run through war-torn, poverty-plagued cities,
throwing great bags full of marble-sized tomatoes
and fist-sized, spotted yellow apples into the streets.
I want this to be the end of need, the end of want.
I want to bring the excessive waters
from the suffering flood victims to the drought-stricken.
I want to save this mad, wasteful profusion
from sinking and vanishing into the dirt, to give it instead
to the hoards of children whose legs
are thinner than pencils, whose bellies
swell out like balloons, with only air.
To the children crowded into cinder-block corners,
clambering over slagheaps, to the children
who are always hungry I want to say,
Here is water, here is food. This is from God-the-abundant,
This is for you, meant for you. Here.
Taste these, eat. Here is plenty of food.

Rubus Fruticosus

Today is the pinnacle day of the year
for blackberries. Today,
today is their moment,
it has to be August, when
those that were silent sing in loud whispers,
and I have ears to hear.
Those that are shy shine black.
They that have so far
hidden under green, hidden in shade
slip onto the stage, into the sun,
and I have eyes to see.
They leap into my bowl.
I thank them. I promise
not to speak of them but in praise.

Post Lapsarian

Through every living spring, I love and fight
the hard earth for my daily bread, for the
sustenance it yields in such mira-
culous response to every newborn prayer
of planted seeds. I gather up those seeds,
I soak them and breathe onto them and plant
them under richest, fullest moonlight and
I water, dance, and sing for them, and chase
away the choking weeds and crows. What I
don't do is drive off to some building, smile
insipid daily greetings at a boss
whom I am certain to forget, whose name,
school, address, forebears, children matter not
one little whit to me, and yes, for that,
I ask to be forgiven. Only that.
Because no disobedience of mine
could force me from all gardens for all time.

Unripe Saints

I am picking blackberries,
thinking of saints, and
considering that moral choices,
moral stands, become inevitable at a certain moment,
like blackberries becoming ripe.
It is not a choice, not really a stand,
it is rather the way that the fruit's colors change on a certain day,
it is simply the direction that the branch bends now,
and you have only to see
what colors have appeared, and what has fallen away—
last year's leaves, perhaps, or a dead branch.
You have only to learn
who has stayed and who has departed.
Some of your childhood will be over forever,
some family and friends will denounce you,
some will die, some will hold their tongues,
some will vanish over the horizon,
and some will rally and remain.
This seems like loyalty or disloyalty.
But it is only inevitable.
Some blackberries are ripe today.
Some will be ripe next week.
Some simply wither and fall.
Some that are ripe and beautiful, I leave untouched,
because I am thinking of bears, and birds, and saints.

Photo by Adam Goldstein.

Because she was first last and always a poet her biography can begin in her words, "I was born on Mount Olympus."

Because she was a spiritually inspired person we can continue her bio with the true story that when as a young teenager she first looked up the hill to see the Parthenon she had an embodied enlightenment experience.

We know that she was also a Phi Beta Kappa student of the Classics and taught Latin for most of the second half of her life.

Because she was by nature a fervent and spiritual universalist she joined what she later came to see as a false religion, the Church of Scientology, in order to save the world, and especially the world of her origins, the elite educated East Coast clan she was born into. Rebecca is listed in the New York City Social Registry.

And because she loved poetry even at the age of 12 she cried and cried while reading first editions of her grandmother's volumes of Edna St. Vincent Millay. She also had a mother who knew intimately the poetic greats of her Vassar generation. Rebecca grew up in a highly literate family with Pulitzer Prize novelists and poets as in-laws and confidants. Remnants of which became a life support gathering after she escaped from the organization of her first religion. Unitarianism became her faith community for the rest of her life. And the mentors of her poetry surrounded her, as did the community of Belfast, the churches and most especially the fellow poets who with merit and appreciation sustained her writing for the dozen years she lived here, until cancer took her life.

Rebecca had children and grandchildren. Her son Adam Goldstein, a writer, Irish Folk singer, entertainer and journalist in Colorado. Her daughter Sheyna Goldstein-Weinstein who is lives in Israel as a convert to Judaism with her family and four children. Her adopted son Justin Phelps who is married and lives in Sweden and has a daughter Astrid. A stepdaughter, Amber Newcomer, who lives in Connecticut, has a daughter Lillian, and is a trained chef.

Rebecca reconnected to her first love, Duncan Newcomer, and they lived together in New Harmony, Indiana, and moved to Belfast, Maine, in 2013. They were married in the Waldo Country General Hospital chapel two months before she died.

Rebecca was exceedingly proud of her poetry, her knowledge and love of Latin, her marriage, her children, and the authenticity of her evolving spiritual life.

—Duncan Newcomer

www.ingramcontent.com/pod-product-compliance
Lightning Source LLC
Chambersburg PA
CBHW030532080526
44586CB00011B/412